All About
SHIPS
AND BOATS

by Rose Cully

illustrated by Ron Mahoney

Harcourt
SCHOOL PUBLISHERS

D1797537

Requests for permission to make copies of any part of the work should be addressed to School Permissions and Copyrights, Harcourt, Inc., 6277 Sea Harbor Drive, Orlando, Florida 32887-6777. Fax: 407-345-2418.

HARCOURT and the Harcourt Logo are trademarks of Harcourt, Inc., registered in the United States of America and/or other jurisdictions.

Printed in China

ISBN 10: 0-15-350327-0
ISBN 13: 978-0-15-350327-6

Ordering Options
ISBN 10: 0-15-349941-9 (Grade 6 ELL Collection)
ISBN 13: 978-0-15-349941-8 (Grade 6 ELL Collection)
ISBN 10: 0-15-357374-0 (package of 5)
ISBN 13: 978-0-15-357374-3 (package of 5)

5 6 7 8 9 10   0940   12 11 10 09

Close your eyes and imagine you are floating on the water in a boat! The motion of the water rocks you back and forth. You can hear the waves gently lapping on the side of your boat. The seabirds fly above you. You can smell the salt air. What kind of boat do you see in your mind? There are many different kinds of boats and ships.

A boat travels on water. A large boat is
called a ship. There are many kinds of boats,
including canoes, rowboats, sailboats, and
motorboats. Tugboats help to pull other boats.
Submarines can travel underwater. Fireboats
put out fires near and on the water.

Boats float and move on water in many different ways. Some boats have one or more oars or paddles. People dip them into the water to move the boat. Examples include canoes, kayaks, or rowboats.

Sailboats have sails that catch the wind to push them along. Other boats have motors or different types of engines. Some boats use a combination of these things.

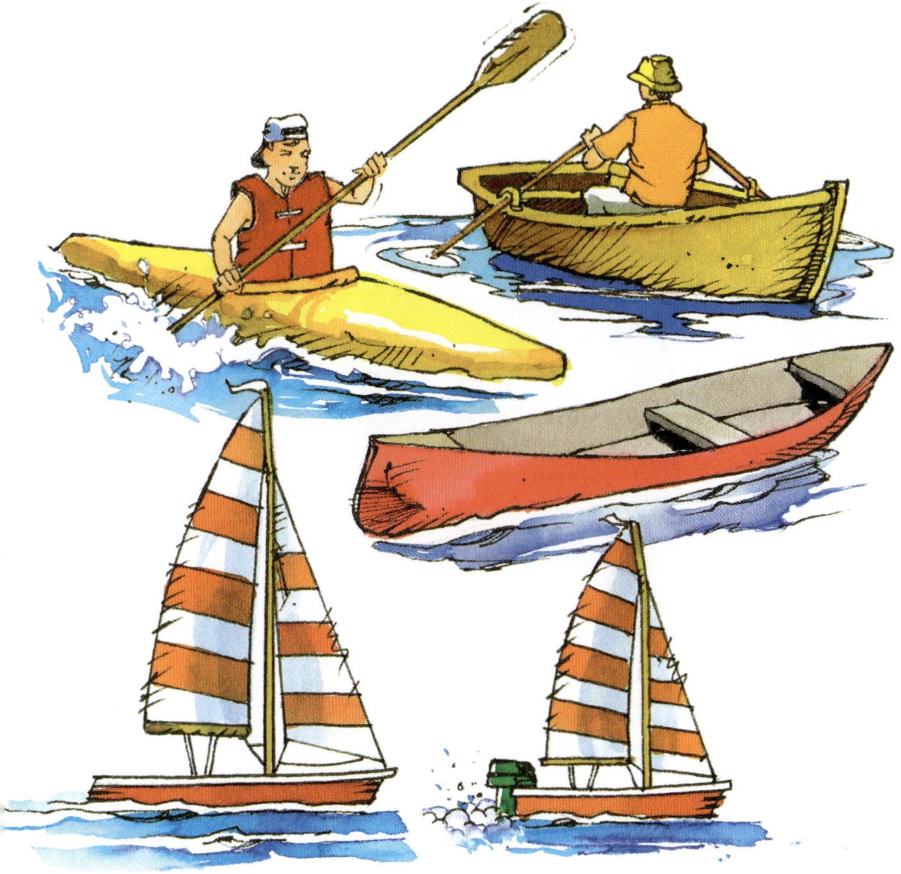

Boats have many parts. When talking about boats, we use special words. The *bow* is the front of the boat, and the *stern* is the back of the boat.

Sometimes you will hear a person refer to the *starboard* side or the *port* side of a boat. The starboard side is the right side, when a person is facing forward on a boat. The port side of a boat is the left side.

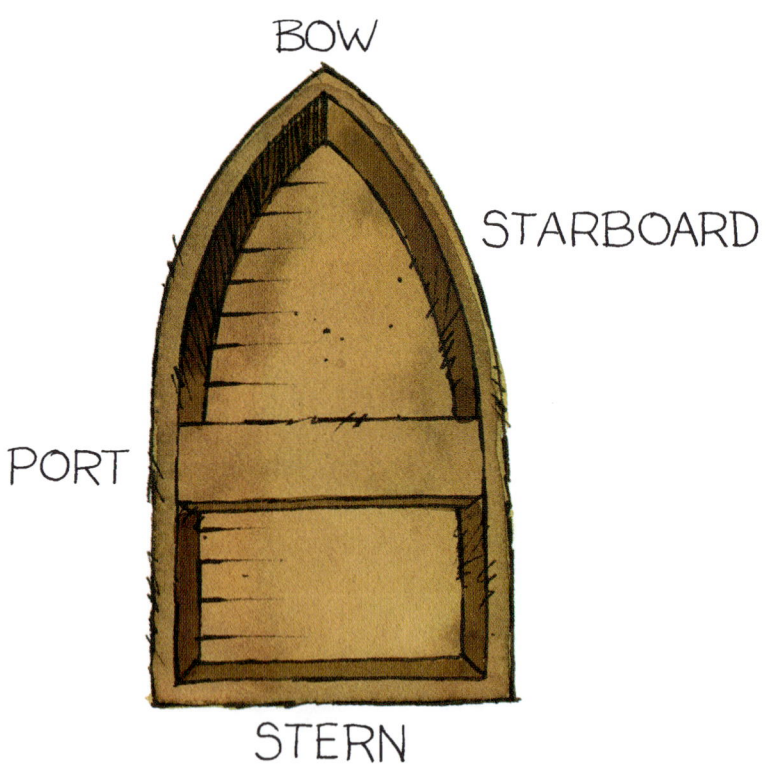

TILLER

MAST

HULL

A *tiller* is a bar, or handle, that is used to change the direction of the boat. The *hull* is the main body of the boat. The *mast* is the pole that holds up the sail of a sailboat. A mast might be very tall. Watching sailors ascend to the very top is an amazing sight.

Some boats may be made from logs. The
simplest kind of boat is a raft. A raft is usually
flat and may just be made of logs tied together.
Native Americans learned how to carve canoes
from hollow trunks of trees, many, many years
ago! Today people still enjoy paddling down
rivers in canoes for fun.

Another early use of boats was in Egypt, around 3000 B.C. The ancient Egyptians used boats for fishing, enjoyment, and travel along the Nile River. The Nile is the longest river in the world. The Egyptians traveled along with the current, or direction of the water.

An ancient Egyptian ship had only one rectangular sail. The ship also had many oars for people to row when they needed to move against the current. The ships were also painted and decorated to look attractive.

The Vikings, ancient people of Scandinavia, lived about 1,200 years ago. They were the first people to make efficient, large ships that could sail long distances.

These ships were made of wood. The wood was waterproofed with a coating of pine tar, a sticky substance from pine trees. Each ship had a single, square sail that was sewn from wool and was brightly colored. The hulls of the Viking ships, also called longships, were curved at the ends and decorated with wood carvings. Viking longships, like the ancient Egyptian ships, had teams of rowers, to make the ships go faster.

Vikings traveled long distances across the water. Sometimes they did not reach their destinations. Dangerous weather and storms could destroy their ships. The Vikings explored many new lands. They were even the first Europeans to come to North America.

In America, in 1769, James Watt patented a steam engine. This was important because people no longer needed to depend on wind or human power to travel long distances by water.

Later Robert Fulton invented the first successful steamboat in America. In 1807, Fulton's first steamboat traveled from New York City to Albany, New York. It traveled a distance of 150 miles (241 km), going at a speed of about five miles (8 km) per hour. This steamboat made regular trips to Albany after the first trip was a success. The boat sometimes carried about a hundred passengers.

Ships are important for us in our world today. Trade among countries depends upon ships. Ships sail around the world to bring food, fuel, and people from one country to another country.

Boats come in all shapes and sizes. Perhaps you have made a toy boat and sailed it in a local pond or fountain. Some young children play with toy boats in the bathtub. Some people make model sailboats out of wood. Some people make toy motorboats that can race! Large or small, boats are a big part of our lives.

Scaffolded Language Development

CATEGORIES OF VEHICLES Learning words by category is a good way to memorize them. Review the meanings of the following words with students. Then have them sort the words into three categories: *boats, land vehicles,* and *flying vehicles.*

bus	helicopter	plane	steamship
canoe	snowmobile	rowboat	submarine
car	jet	sailboat	truck
glider	motorcycle	spaceship	tugboat

When students are finished sorting the words, you may wish to play a guessing game. Students can take turns giving clues about a vehicle. Other students can guess the vehicle.

Science

Imagining Boats Have small groups of students each design a boat based on what they have learned about boats. Have the groups illustrate and write the purpose for their boat. Then have each group present its boat to the class.

School-Home Connection
Boating Experiences Ask students to discuss with their family members the different kinds of boats they have seen or been on.

Word Count: 795